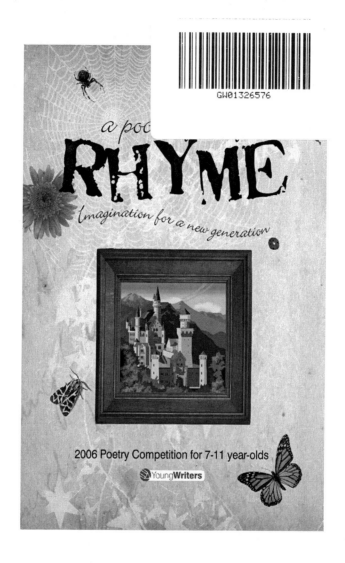

Oxfordshire
Edited by Allison Dowse

First published in Great Britain in 2006 by:
Young Writers
Remus House
Coltsfoot Drive
Peterborough
PE2 9JX
Telephone: 01733 890066
Website: www.youngwriters.co.uk

All Rights Reserved

© Copyright Contributors 2006

SB ISBN 1 84602 476 5

Foreword

Young Writers was established in 1991 and has been passionately devoted to the promotion of reading and writing in children and young adults ever since. The quest continues today. Young Writers remains as committed to the nurturing of poetic and literary talent as ever.

This year's Young Writers competition has proven as vibrant and dynamic as ever and we are delighted to present a showcase of the best poetry from across the UK and in some cases overseas. Each poem has been selected from a wealth of *A Pocketful Of Rhyme* entries before ultimately being published in this, our fourteenth primary school poetry series.

Once again, we have been supremely impressed by the overall quality of the entries we have received. The imagination, energy and creativity which has gone into each young writer's entry made choosing the poems a challenging and often difficult but ultimately hugely rewarding task - the general high standard of the work submitted ensured this opportunity to bring their poetry to a larger appreciative audience.

We sincerely hope you are pleased with this final collection and that you will enjoy *A Pocketful Of Rhyme Oxfordshire* for many years to come.

Contents

Burford Primary School
Kyle Rustage (10)	1
Kate Hoggett (10)	2
Billie Cox & Poppie Baker Smith (10)	3
Adam Bufton (9)	4
Bryony Gibbs (11)	5

Chadlington CE Primary School
Charlotte Whalley (11)	6
Ross Southey (10)	7
Joe Yapp (9)	8
Charlotte Alsop (10)	9
Emma Hutchings (11)	10
Stephen Howard (9)	11
Sam Stevens (10)	12
Ella Blackwell (10)	13

Charlton Primary School
Verity Steele (10)	14
Carys Allott (10)	15
Emma Leader (10)	16
Aiden Collins (11)	17
Clara Hallam (10)	18
Chloe Hobbs-Draper (11)	20
Heather Robertson (11)	21
Ceri Owen (10)	22
Jessica Strickland (9)	23
Oliver Base (9)	24

Glory Farm Primary School
William Jordan (8)	25
Christopher Guttridge (8)	26
David McMillan (8)	27
Ryan Cook (7)	28
Verity Holbem (7)	29
Harry Grundy (8)	30
Jamie Jordan (8)	31

James Titchener (7)	32
Cavan Scoffin-Thomas (8)	33
Gemma Castle (7)	34
Chloe Howlett (7)	35
Fern-Leigh Smith (8)	36
Katy Framingham (7)	37
Millie McGregor (7)	38
Sam Jordan (8)	39
Charlotte Ette (10)	40
Misha Staples (10)	41
Fern Davis (10)	42

Great Rollright Primary School

Georgie Sabin (10)	43
Sophie Napier (10)	44
James Hastings (9)	45

Hagbourne CE Primary School

David Stevens (10)	46
Sophie Shuttler & Jodie Harris (9)	47
Heather Sutherland (9)	48
Rebecca Anne Sutherland (10)	49
Ellie McCarthy (10)	50
Lauren Morgan (9)	51
Rosie Stainthorp (9)	52
Eleanor Suter (9)	53

Harriers Ground Primary School

Kayleigh Saunders (11)	54
Katie Perring (9)	55
Haalah Karim (10)	56
Conor Man McLennan (10)	57
Adam Sullivan (10)	58
Joe McNally (10)	59
Cameron Lambert (11)	60
Zoe Samantha Moore (10)	61
Nat Bagnall (9)	62
Amelia Macmillan (10)	63

Kingham Primary School
    Elizabeth Shelmerdine (9) — 64
    Jonathan Shelmerdine (10) — 65

Lewknor Primary School
    Ben Marsh (8) — 66
    Will Rose (8) — 67
    Nicholas Greaves (9) — 68
    Hamish Bowie (8) — 69
    James Stoddart (10) — 70
    Rebecca Davies (8) — 71
    Daniel Lamb (9) — 72
    Laura Swain (8) — 73
    Ben McIntosh (8) — 74
    Jack McIntosh (10) — 75
    Holly Sutton (10) — 76
    Lucy Vaughan (9) — 77
    Dominic James Savin (9) — 78
    Lily-May Anson (11) — 79
    Lyla Fibert (9) — 80
    Deacon Ashworth (10) — 81
    Charlotte Coles (9) — 82
    Megan Hawkes (10) — 83
    Gemma Sutton (8) — 84
    Amy Miles (11) — 85
    Georgia Rose Morrow (8) — 86
    Adam Muttitt (11) — 87
    Elisabeth J Gowens (10) — 88
    Isabella Carroll (9) — 89

Manor Primary School
    Hollie Harrison (10) — 90
    Gabriel Naughton (11) — 91
    Rosie Darby (10) — 92
    Fráe Mary Elford Bennett (11) — 93
    Jamie Blair (11) — 94
    Alice Strange (11) — 95
    Elizabeth Alcock (10) — 96
    Ruby Livesey (10) — 97
    Jake Bristow (10) — 98

Fern Holliday (11)	99
Katie Payne (11)	100
Lewis Miltenberger (11)	101
Sam Keogh (10)	102
Robert Pocock (11)	103
Annie Royal (10)	104
Christopher Dalley (10)	105
Olivia Jones (10)	106

Marcham Primary School

Matthew Allison (10)	107
Robin Butt (10)	108
Robert Gresham (9)	109
Ben Ireson (9)	110
Jamie Saulter (10)	111
Harriet Scott (9)	112
George Newman (10)	113
Kieran Belcher (8)	114
Aleisha Fraser (9)	115
Sarah Tierney (8)	116
Louis Jackson (8)	117

Moulsford Preparatory School

Freddie O'Donald (9)	118
Freddie Carr (9)	119
Tristan Benfield (9)	120
Ed Howlett (9)	121
George Buckley (9)	122
Jordy Williams (10)	123
Max Hearnden (9)	124
Mike Garside (9)	125
Conor Anderson (9)	126
Alex Butt (9)	127
Daniel Watts (10)	128
William Ottosson (10)	129
Henry Graham (10)	130
Alex Harmer (11)	131
Toby Stoddart (11)	132
Henry Ellis (10)	133
Karl Simmons (11)	134

Jack Maple (10)	135
Trevor Warner (10)	136
Toby Worrall Thompson (10)	137
Patrick Lawson Statham (10)	138
Ben West (10)	139
Leo Wood (10)	140
Tom Godfrey (10)	141
Toby Marlow (11)	142
James Fotherby (8)	143
Hamish Veitch (8)	144
Joe Ellis (8)	145
Ollie Butt (11)	146
Henry Binning (11)	147
James Bywater (11)	148
Jacob Simons (11)	149
David Wheatley (11)	150
Phin Leslau (10)	151
Sam Lerche-Thomsen (10)	152
Louis Allen (11)	153
William Flindall (11)	154
George Carr (11)	155
Charlie Mansfield (11)	156
March Showering Russell (10)	157
Jonathan Deacon (10)	158
Hugh Barklem (10)	159
JJ Sermon (8)	160
Rupert Boddington (10)	161
Henrik Cox (10)	162
Jamie Chapman (9)	163
Nicholas Bryan (10)	164
Harry Stott (10)	165
Tobias Whetton (9)	166
Joe Tollet (10)	167
William McDermott (9)	168
Alex Andrews (10)	169
Benedict Rothschild (10)	170
Sam Jones (10)	171

Orchard Close, Sibford School

Rebecca Bonham (8)	172
Harry Little (9)	173

James Paton (9)	174
Jack Robins (9)	175
Lali Slade (9)	176
Henry Wood (9)	177
Charlotte Jayne Harrison (10)	178
Jake Mayo (10)	179
Barney Cremin (10)	180
Lucy Steel (10)	181
Jacob Bearman (10)	182
Kate Bowen (10)	183
Helen Bonham (8)	184
Katherine Bell (8)	185
William Harrison (8)	186
Henry Moore (10)	187
John Rafter-Tunnicliffe (9)	188

Radley CE Primary School

Jack Corrigan (8)	189
Vicky Paige (7)	190
Cara Doherty (9)	191
Chloe Busby (7)	192
Bethan Rae Reeves Long (9)	193
Thomas Harris (9)	194
Jonathan Charalambous (8)	195
Harvey Ball (9)	196
Harry Sudworth (8)	197
Kyle Kerby (8)	198
Conor Mosedale (7)	199

St Leonard's Primary School, Banbury

Rory McLaughlin (10)	200
Anna Holmes & Elise Cole (9)	201
Isabel Stafford (10)	202
Chantelle Merry-Taylor (10)	203
Emma Shaw (10)	204
Hasib Iqbal (11)	205
Sophie Louise McNally (9)	206
Bethany Packham (9)	207
Harry O'Sullivan (9)	208
Adam Bushell (11)	209

Matthew Hawtin (10)   210
Ashley Keyes (9)   211
Joshua Kerby (11)   212

The Poems

Love

Love is pink like a nice sunny day.
Love sounds like joy and happiness.
Love tastes like a scrumptious chocolate smoothie.
Love smells like a newly grown rose.
Love feels like it's another day.
Love looks like a beautiful princess.
Love reminds me of friendship.

Kyle Rustage (10)
Burford Primary School

Happiness

Happiness smells like hot cross buns.
Happiness is yellow like a big hot sun.
Happiness sounds like laughter in the air.
Happiness tastes like chocolate melting on your tongue.
Happiness looks like a big bright sunflower.
Happiness reminds me of a big bowl of Smarties.
Happiness feels like you've got butterflies in your tummy.

Kate Hoggett (10)
Burford Primary School

All About Fun

Fun is like a multicoloured rainbow.
Fun sounds like a party and a disco.
Fun tastes like chocolate cake with extra chocolate
                               with marshmallows and fudge.
Fun feels like laughing out of breath.
Fun looks like smiles full of laughter.
Fun reminds me of my friends.

Billie Cox & Poppie Baker Smith (10)
Burford Primary School

My Dog

My dog her name is Zoe
And she is only three,
She often likes to jump up
And sit upon my knee.

Her eyes are brown and shiny,
She likes to run around,
She often likes to bury her bone
Way deep into the ground.

I love my dog so much,
She means everything to me,
She sleeps upon my bed
And keeps me company.

Adam Bufton (9)
Burford Primary School

Anger

Anger is black like a dark, gloomy hole.
Anger sounds like thunder beating the air,
Anger tastes like a dark sour lemon melting in your mouth,
Anger smells like a turkey burning in the oven,
Anger feels like a prickly porcupine,
Anger looks like a funeral taking place,
Anger reminds me of fighting.

Bryony Gibbs (11)
Burford Primary School

Fire From Hell

I could see it,
I could feel it,
I could hear it,
I was there.
All I could see was fire.
All I could hear was screaming,
I thought I was dreaming,
How wrong I was.
I could see it,
I could feel it,
I could hear it,
I was there.

The screaming became louder as I walked,
I started to mumble and talk,
How wrong I was.
I could see it,
I could feel it,
I could hear it,
I was there.

How I was running,
As I would talk,
Someone was watching like a hawk.
How wrong I was.
I could see it,
I could feel it,
I could hear it,
I was there.

How wrong I was.
It wasn't someone watching
It was something,
As I would call it . . . 'fire from Hell'!
I could see it,
I could feel it,
I could hear it,
I was there.

Charlotte Whalley (11)
Chadlington CE Primary School

Drunk Running

Hi I'm Frisky
I'm incredibly drunk
Drunk a bottle of Scottish whisky
I'm running home
Can't see good, all gone blurry, feel like foam!
Thud!
I'm on the floor now at a very low height
Head's bleeding
Night . . . a night-night.

Ross Southey (10)
Chadlington CE Primary School

Football

I walk onto the pitch,
As ready as a dog
I feel very confident
And my walk's turning into a jog.

I see Harry kick the ball to me
So I dribble up the pitch
I kick the ball straight into the net
And walk straight into a ditch.

I hear the crowd go wild
I'm covered in lots of mud
I'm really, really tired
So I fall to the ground with a thud!

Joe Yapp (9)
Chadlington CE Primary School

The Butterfly

You fly so gracefully
You're as soft as a rose
When you find a flower
How gently you pose.

Flutterby butterfly
Flutter by me
Flutterby butterfly
Flutter for me

Tell me where
Oh where do you go?
Tell me now
I'll fly with you so.

Flutterby butterfly
Flutter by me
Flutterby butterfly
Flutter for me

You are pink, blue and white
Your wings are as thin as glass
Your body as delicate as a diamond
There you are in the clover in the grass.

Flutterby butterfly
Flutter by me
Flutterby butterfly
Flutter for me.

Charlotte Alsop (10)
Chadlington CE Primary School

Water

I get ready
I wobble
'On your marks!
Go, go!'

I dive in
The water swallows me up
I come up to the surface
I breathe.

I'm going down the pool
Are people cheering?
They must be
Charlotte's there.

My arms go fast
I kick like mad
I hear people cheering
The end.

I got a trophy
And a medal
Everyone's cheering
I've won!

Emma Hutchings (11)
Chadlington CE Primary School

Guess What?

I went to a match
With my mum and dad
I didn't like it
Cause my dad went mad.

When I got there
I bought a programme
Then my dad looked through
And guess what Dad said? 'Hey who's Mr Sam?'

Then the match started
It was Liverpool v Chelsea
Chelsea scored
And guess what? Dad spilt his tea on me.

Now it's half time
'Nothing can happen now,' I said
I went to the loo
And guess what my dad said? 'I've got a toy called Mr Ted!'

After half time
We went back to the stand
Liverpool scored
And guess what? Dad went mad.

Then Liverpool scored again
It was 2-1 now
The game was over
And now it was time to say ciâo.

Stephen Howard (9)
Chadlington CE Primary School

Is This The War?

In the tomb thousands of metres underground
It's pitch-black, black as midnight.
I step on a rock and know the predators are alert.
I'm deep in their tomb.
I hear a noise.
The doors are closing,
They've trapped us, we're in the middle of a war.
The war of the alien and the predator.
I hear a scream,
It tells me to get out.
I run then I hear it, the predator,
I run but it catches me,
Is this the end of me? I think.
It stops, just then it realises I've chosen my side
The side of the predator!

Sam Stevens (10)
Chadlington CE Primary School

My Dog Poppy

My dog's name is Poppy,
She plays with me,
I love her very much
And she loves her tea.

My dog Poppy she's ten years old,
She plays with me
And does what she's told.

My dog Poppy her fur's so soft,
I'll feel so sad when she dies
But that's a long time off.

My dog Poppy she's ten years old,
She plays with me
And does what she's told.

My dog Poppy I hear her bark at me,
She scratches at the gate
And barks at the sea.
I put her on the gravel
To have a fun around,
She didn't like it and went back to the house.

My dog Poppy she's ten years old,
She plays with me
And does what she's told.

Ella Blackwell (10)
Chadlington CE Primary School

Summer - Cinquain

Hot days
Bees are buzzing
Sunbathe in the garden
Squirt Mum with a water pistol
Summer.

Verity Steele (10)
Charlton Primary School

Sweet Shop

Bonbons, chocolate, sugar and more,
The sweet shop is a great, cool store.
The shelves stacked high with wonderful treats,
All for me to share and eat.
Lollipops sour,
Boiled sweets have got the power,
I think I had better stop
Before I go *pop!*

Carys Allott (10)
Charlton Primary School

The Butterfly

Silently, oh how silently,
The butterfly swoops through the misty air,
Its beautiful colours glistening,
Without a single care.
Most delicate animal of the land,
In every country it will fly,
Wings flapping freely,
In the brightening blue sky.
Trying to find the perfect flower,
To sit on for the hour,
Sucking carelessly on nectar,
To regain its power,
Silently, oh how silently.

Emma Leader (10)
Charlton Primary School

The Werewolf

The werewolf comes out at night
He gives kids massive bites
In the morning your parents see a flood
But it's not water, it's blood
'Argh!' screams your mum
When she sees that massive mark on your tongue
The police are thinking, *what a crime*
But it's happened again at the same time
Then one night at Stone Henge
The humans were planning for revenge
Then out of nowhere the werewolf came
But the human people forced him pain
They had shot him down with a machine gun
And straight away went to the café for a bun
It was the end of the werewolf tribe
And in the newspaper they had a jibe
But this was not the end
As the werewolf could be round the bend . . .

Aiden Collins (11)
Charlton Primary School

The Trap

Clatter, bang, roar, crunch
The motorbike was near
The man was a coming
And soon he would be here

He rode his motorcycle
To the moonlit door
Then knocked on the dirty boards
Much older than before

But there was no answer
To that hip hop man
Sitting on his bike there
Drinking out of his cola can

He stopped his engine
And got off his bike
When he went round the side
Which would cost him his life

As you see it was a trap
For that poor old dude
With his funky hat
He was certainly screwed

The trap went very wrong
And when the boot came down
It hit him in the head
And he started to see clowns

He then fell over
And bashed his head
Then started to scream
'I want to go to bed!'

He closed his eyes
And let out a sigh
'I wish I was dead,'
He said to the sky

He rolled over
Hitting the trigger of his gun
Closed his eye as the bullet fired
'Goodbye to the world, goodbye to my mum.'

Clara Hallam (10)
Charlton Primary School

School Day

The school day begins
a long day ahead
I know where I'd be
and that's in my bed

Time for assembly
all gathered in the hall
it would be much more fun
out playing with a ball

Time for a break
we're playing around
Mrs Irwin's computer
is out of bounds

A maths lesson next
a subject I hate
we'll work together
me and my mate

Sandwiches and crisps
I have for lunch
Water to drink
And an apple to crunch

Painting and drawing
the things I do best
much much better
than a spelling test

I've finished my lessons
done all I can do
time to clean up
and say goodbye to you

Mum's outside
waiting to see
if we've had a good day
my sister and me.

Chloe Hobbs-Draper (11)
Charlton Primary School

Stray Dog

His eyes are staring longingly up at you,
Hoping for a morsel of food.
The pads on his paws are raw and pink,
His coat has lost its shine.
His body so weak and fragile
That you can tell that he is a stray dog.

Heather Robertson (11)
Charlton Primary School

Seasons

The bitter cold,
All is white and bold.
Australia is hot,
Here is not!

Blossoms on trees,
Warmed up knees.
The sun has come,
Toes aren't numb!

The hot sun,
People having fun.
Ice-cold lollipops,
Cold air in all the shops!

The golden leaves
Fall off the trees.
Winter is near,
Different sounds you can hear!

Ceri Owen (10)
Charlton Primary School

What Is A Gorilla?

A hairy thing,
A jungle king.

A tree swinger,
A good clinger.

A banana eater,
A chest beater.

A big monkey,
A bit funky.

A huge beast,
A banana feast.

A bent back,
A brown sack.

Jessica Strickland (9)
Charlton Primary School

Rocket

Our food supply levels are falling
Our oxygen dangerously low
The boosters are rapidly waving
And the inside's beginning to show

We've been sent on a terrible journey
To fly there and back from Mars
It's the first time I've ever been up here
And the asteroids the size of cars!

The atmosphere of Earth is nearing
We're prepared for the terrible bash
Our mouths are shaking like crazy,
And then suddenly . . . *crash!*

But we were ready for the landing
Our seat belts securely done
We hop out of the rocket laughing,
'*Wow!* That was good fun!'

Oliver Base (9)
Charlton Primary School

The Dragon's Den

There was once a green dragon called Drago,
He lived alone in a cave,
He was a friendly dragon
And his best friend was called Dave.

Dave would come for his tea,
Their favourite food was burnt marshmallow on a stick,
Which they gobbled up,
With one big lick.

Drago and Dave liked to play,
Their favourite game was hide-and-seek,
Dave would hide
And Drago would peek!

William Jordan (8)
Glory Farm Primary School

Barney

Soft and silky
Fun and furry
Loves to play and hops all day
He can't sketch
Loves to fetch
Barney likes to have a good time
That's the end of my rhyme.

Christopher Guttridge (8)
Glory Farm Primary School

Porsches

I like cars very much
A Porsche is the best
Red, black, silver too
I'll wait till I pass my test!

My mum says they are lovely
My dad says, 'Cor it's great!'
My brother says, 'Let's get one!'
I suppose I'll have to wait!

David McMillan (8)
Glory Farm Primary School

Monsters

Monsters are always scary
Monsters are sometimes hairy

Monsters can be big or small
Some monsters can climb up the wall

Red, yellow, green or blue
They all like to try to scare you

Monsters can live anywhere
Some monsters live at the fair.

Ryan Cook (7)
Glory Farm Primary School

My Two Brothers

I've got two brothers
They are very special to me
One is much taller than me
And the other is much smaller than me
I look up to my big brother
My little brother looks up to me
My big brother helps me on the computer
My little brother wants to play
My big brother helps me with my homework
My little brother wants to play!
My big brother helps me on the PlayStation
My little brother wants to play!
My big brother helps me on my bike
My little brother wants to play!
I have two brothers, they both mean the world to me
I wouldn't change them, but for Christmas
I really would like a sister!

Verity Holbem (7)
Glory Farm Primary School

The Skeleton

I am a skeleton
My bones are white
I shine in the dark
And I glow in the night

So don't look to see me
When you go to bed
Just pull up your blanket
Right over your head.

Harry Grundy (8)
Glory Farm Primary School

The Ghostly King

King Harry III was a ghost,
His robes were red and gold,
His shoes were made of black leather
And his face was mean and cold.

King Harry III had an army,
Of Vikings and of knights,
His army was tough and mean
And were always looking for fights!

King Harry III had an enemy,
His name was King Arthur VII,
They had had many battles,
There were up to the eleventh.

King Harry III had lost an eye,
The battle had been very bad,
King Harry was very cross,
But King Arthur was very glad!

Jamie Jordan (8)
Glory Farm Primary School

Blue And Black

Blue is bright, black is dark
Blue and black are my favourite colours.
The sky is blue,
The sky is big.
The night is black,
The night sky is scary.
A snooker ball is blue,
A snooker ball is shiny.
A PlayStation is black,
A PlayStation is cool.
Blu-tack is blue,
Blu-tack is sticky.
My wallet is black,
My wallet keeps money.
My Game Boy is blue,
My Game Boy is fun.
Blue is bright, black is dark,
Blue and black are my favourite colours.

James Titchener (7)
Glory Farm Primary School

My Naughty Little Sister

I have a little sister
Who's naughty through and through
She creeps up behind me
And then shouts, 'Boo!'

She likes to give me a pinch
Just around the waist
Then at dinnertime
She likes to burp in my face

But the funny thing is you see
My mum says the naughty one
Really is *me!*

Cavan Scoffin-Thomas (8)
Glory Farm Primary School

A Pony

Ginger was a pony, ten years old.
She galloped round the field
And never got cold.
Ginger loved to race every single day
And when she won she swished her tail
And ate lots of hay.

Gemma Castle (7)
Glory Farm Primary School

My Teacher Poem

T eachers are small, teachers are tall
E very teacher likes us all
A t times they're funny and make us laugh
C hloe goes to Mrs Stevenson's class
H appy times at school
E ven when I'm not feeling cool
R unning around the playground having fun
S chool and teachers are here to stay, to help us do our best!

Chloe Howlett (7)
Glory Farm Primary School

Food

Some food is good for you
Some food is bad
I would like to eat lots of chocolate
And that would make my mum *mad!*
I eat all of my vegetables
That are put on my plate
So I stay healthy and always feel *great!*

Fern-Leigh Smith (8)
Glory Farm Primary School

Boots

My pet cat Boots
Is black and white
And the other day he gave us
Such a big fright.

He brought a live mouse into our house,
Daddy was away
And Mummy had to think hard,
But she rescued the mouse
With a bowl and some card.

She then took the mouse,
Out of our house
And let it go in our front yard.

Katy Framingham (7)
Glory Farm Primary School

Seaside

Watching the sea splash in and out
Feel the sunshine gazing upon us
You can get ice creams
Strawberry, vanilla and chocolate
Yum! Yum! Yum!
Get on your suit and join in
By coming in and swim
Splash! Splosh!
Soak everyone that you know
See the sand swirling around us
Watch the dolphins jump out from under the water
Listen to people scratching and shouting
Watch everyone dancing around
Children digging with spades and building sandcastles with buckets
Relaxing under the huge parasols
Burgers are near, come on! Eat one!
Sea is blue and green, sometimes darker
Feel the pop fizzling down your throat
Watch the whole beach get covered over with the sea.

Millie McGregor (7)
Glory Farm Primary School

Alien Teacher

My teacher is an alien,
His name is Mr Bean,
He sets us loads of homework,
Which I think is very mean!

We know he is an alien,
Cos of his green tentacles and gigantic toes,
His one eye
And his big red nose!

Some of his classes are fun,
But some of them are mean,
The worst part of the day is lunch,
Cos he makes us eat our veggies green!

Sam Jordan (8)
Glory Farm Primary School

Love In A Box

I'm packing my box but I wish I could
put something other than toys in.

I wish that I could reach in my heart
and pull out lots of love and put it in
the biggest box in the world.

I wish that hope came in a jar
and I would put gallons of it in a huge box.

I wish that happiness was floating around the universe
and you could just reach up and grab a handful

I wish that trust was like an elastic band
and you could stretch it so big it would fit round
each little body that walks the Earth.

I wish that joy was Russia but bigger,
so big it does not even fit in a box.

I wish that every feeling that's in my heart
could be sent to people all over the world
in a special box.

Charlotte Ette (10)
Glory Farm Primary School

Love In A Box

If I could put something in a box instead of toys
I would put in love, so you have care.
If I could put something in a box instead of clothes
I would put in joy so you can celebrate.
If I could put something in a box instead of a toothbrush
I would put in happiness so you can be happy.
If I could put something in a box
I would put in everything for you so you'll always be happy.

Misha Staples (10)
Glory Farm Primary School

Love In A Box

I would put in a big hug, a hug full of happiness.
If there was something I could do I would give love,
Love that they need,
Friendship, I could be their friend every year,
All year caring and kindness then your dream will come true.
Hope and wishes will come out of that box.
Your hope is in there.
Things you need you will find.
Just trust the box.

Fern Davis (10)
Glory Farm Primary School

Uh-Oh

Middle of the night, the lights are out,
I wake up.
My heater has been left on,
It is boiling, I am thirsty.
I get out of bed, my eyes wincing in the darkness.
Over the toy-covered floor,
Tiptoe to the door, grab the handle then pull! *Creak!*
Uh-oh . . . murmur, snore . . . *Phew.*
Tiptoe, tiptoe,
I'm in the hall now.
Tiptoe,
Bump! Ouch! I've fallen over something.
Quick, to the door.
I stand up quietly and run through
And there are the stairs.
Down, down, down - as if I was entering the middle of the Earth.
Oh no, I've trodden on a squeaky toy *sque-sshh . . . !*
Murmur, murmur, snore.
I jump down the final few steps, *'Ouch!'*
I've hit the ceiling.
Go down the final step, slowly rubbing my head.
Here's the living room, the fire still blazing.
But the cold stone is freezing,
Quick, *run* to the kitchen!
I end up drinking three bottles of water and using two plasters,
I even fall asleep in front of the fire
then . . . *'Cockadoodledoo!'*
Uh-oh.

Georgie Sabin (10)
Great Rollright Primary School

Zoo

When my brother was two,
He went to the zoo,
Where there were monkeys,
Camels and much more too,
He had his dummy in his mouth
And was as happy as could be.
My mum got him a chocolate cupcake
From the little cake store,
Mmmm
And they went to see the monkeys,
Tom then just looked and looked
And laughed at the monkeys
As they climbed the trees.
Then as quick as lightning,
My mum took his dummy out of his mouth
And put it in the bin,
Never to be seen again!
And ever since,
My mum has said,
'It got eaten by the kangaroo!'

Sophie Napier (10)
Great Rollright Primary School

5 Squirrels

5 squirrels sitting in a tree,
4 of them fell off Mum's knee,
3 went to hospital and had stitches in their head,
2 of those squirrels had to stay in bed,
1 little squirrel sitting on Mum's knee,
He fell off and it ended in a catastrophe!

James Hastings (9)
Great Rollright Primary School

The Path Of Love

If to complete each task
It's like following a path
If you're stuck or something
Think of something like a calf
Or choose a nice colour
Like white on a dove
So get on the right track
And think of something like love
Try to do your best
And sniff up the trail
And think of something wonderful
Like a lovely shell on a snail
Because love is important
It is all around
If there's one thing love can do
It makes the world go round.

David Stevens (10)
Hagbourne CE Primary School

On The Day I Was Born

On the day I was born
I saw a glint of light.

On the day I was born
There was more love in the world.

On the day I was born
I saw the sun and moon.

On the day I was born
There were more people added to the world.

Sophie Shuttler & Jodie Harris (9)
Hagbourne CE Primary School

When I Fell In Love

On the day the world began
I was nothing at all
On the day the grass grew
Animals came to you
On the day I crawled
I said my first word
On the day I was born
I saw the world
On the day I was in love
I was a new girl.

Heather Sutherland (9)
Hagbourne CE Primary School

The Panther

Clawing the bars,
Of a lonely cage,
No space to walk,
No room for rage.

Clawing the bars,
Desperate for the plain,
Desperate for the jungle,
Can feel only pain.

Clawing the bars,
Alone with thoughts and aching feet,
Dreaming of food,
Dreaming of meat.

Clawing the bars,
In the hull of a ship,
On the back of a plane,
With the crack of a whip.

Clawing the bars,
Bright hazel eyes,
Turn to a muddy brown,
As slowly she dies.

Rebecca Anne Sutherland (10)
Hagbourne CE Primary School

My Family

My dad is
a cool dad,
a funny dad,
a rock and roll
kind of dad!

My mum is
a funky mum,
a caring mum,
an out and about
kind of mum!

My brother is
a laughing brother,
a thoughtful brother,
a football mad
kind of brother!

My dog is
a mad dog,
a happy dog,
a can you come and play with me
kind of dog!

My cat is
a lazy cat,
a pretty cat,
a can I have my dinner
kind of cat!

And this mad and wonderful family is mine, all mine!

Ellie McCarthy (10)
Hagbourne CE Primary School

On The Day I Started School

On the day I started school
I ate lots of gruel.

We were sharing all day long
But I was still a little scared.

I was funny, I was happy
I was as merry as a lark.

I was happy when it was home time
So I laughed all the way home!

Lauren Morgan (9)
Hagbourne CE Primary School

The Hen

There once was a boy named Ben,
Who looked a bit like a hen,
He went to Belize
And caught a disease
And is now working in a pen!

Rosie Stainthorp (9)
Hagbourne CE Primary School

Sick

Ian's got a lurgy,
Mandy's got the flu,
Half the class are off with colds,
What a to-do!

Sophie's feeling funny,
Helen's got a bug,
Teacher of course all snug in bed,
Drinking cocoa from a mug!

Sitting at my desk now,
Watching Mrs King,
When Lucy runs off looking green,
Oh, the poor, poor thing!

Sitting on the sofa,
Watching Jackie Chan,
School called off today,
Mum says,
They've run out of substitutes!

Eleanor Suter (9)
Hagbourne CE Primary School

Sweets

Lollipops, bubblegum and chocolate too
Lots of sweets for me and you
Candyfloss, sugar balls and we chew and eat
And when you taste it, it tastes so sweet
And they're wrapped up so neat
Chocolate eggs and sugary sweets
All of them are all for me.

Kayleigh Saunders (11)
Harriers Ground Primary School

Birthday

B iscuit at the party bash
I ce-cold drinks
R ound the bend people come
T aking poems to put into books
H ello to the other people
D inner on the table
A ny cake left?
Y ellow lemons on the side of the glasses.

Katie Perring (9)
Harriers Ground Primary School

The Sweet Shop!

I own a sweet shop
With loads of lollipops
Chocolate and sweets
Don't drop them on the street
Here comes a lady, I wonder who she is
Oh I know you, you're Liz
Come in here my friend, sweets for you
I'll give you a triple chocolate goo
Bye-bye see you again soon
'No thanks, those chocolates were awful!'

Haalah Karim (10)
Harriers Ground Primary School

My Brother

J amie's annoying
A nd he's always teasing me
M e and Jamie always argue all of the time
I always try to ignore him
E ardrums bursting everywhere because we argue!

Conor Man McLennan (10)
Harriers Ground Primary School

The Nail-Biting Cup Tie

At the start of the cup tie the players walk on,
Onto the pitch to their favourite club song.

The mascots run out onto the pitch and onto the green, green grass,
As the ref walks out from the tunnel as this game might be his last.

The home team shake hands with the away team in the centre circle,
The home in blue and away in green and the goalies white and purple.

The game kicks off with the green team who give the ball away,
The home take possession and run the other way.

The half time break is nearing and the score is still 0-0
And green put it out for a throw-in and blue moves in for the kill.

Half time break is coming and the crowd are throwing apple cores,
Then suddenly a green breaks and runs up the pitch and scores!

Suddenly the whistle goes and the greens are one-nil up,
Down goes the manager into the tunnel to fill his cup.

Out come the players for the second half,
For the greens it's one great big laugh.

Blue take the ball, down the right-hand side,
Johnny puts the cross in and Peter heads it wide.

Suddenly he commits a foul
And a player goes and gets a towel.

The ref reaches for his pocket, this is going to be hard,
Yes it is, it's a red card.

Johnny pops up for the penalty because he's going to take,
Surely this is going to be a piece of cake.

Yes he tucks it in the corner nowhere near the keeper,
He went the wrong way, should have been a leaper.

Waiting for the whistle the crowd start to sing,
Hitting the bar and rebounding in.

The final whistle goes and the blues take the cup,
But greens are so full of jealousy that they had given up.

Adam Sullivan (10)
Harriers Ground Primary School

Fast Food

F ast food runs away
A t the bottom of my plate
S ome of it I quite enjoy
T ime again I like McCoy's

F ood, food is very nice
O n my plate I like some rice
O n my plate I like some sauce
D o it mostly by myself, I make a second course.

Joe McNally (10)
Harriers Ground Primary School

Anger!

Hate, anger, rage builds up inside,
When you're angry you push your other feelings aside.
You feel so mad you feel like steam is coming out of your ears,
It feels so horrible you might burst into tears.
People make fun of what you do
And they would never know that you were there,
But you stuck their bums to the chairs.
Next time bullies go and steal your lunch,
Tell them off, but don't give 'em a punch.

Cameron Lambert (11)
Harriers Ground Primary School

Hallowe'en Poem

Hallowe'en is the time for ghosts and ghouls,
And they use skulls for footballs.

Hallowe'en is in October,
When they drink they all get sober.

Hallowe'en makes you feel so dandy,
All you can do is eat candy.

Spiders spin their webs so bright,
Witches cackle in the night.

Witch's cauldron with such a fright
And her spells run away through the night.

Zoe Samantha Moore (10)
Harriers Ground Primary School

The Big Match

E ngland smack that ball in that net
N orthern Ireland Vs England
G ermany giggle while England play
L iving the life as a football player
A re Brazil the best in the world?
N orthern Ireland are history
D irty slide tackles from Brazil

F ranky hits the far post
O n the volley Rooney
O *oooh!*
T ick-tock, five more minutes
B ecks braces himself
A nd the crowd goes wild
L ovely skill by Becks
L ike the throw by Gary Neville

T eam tactics in the changing rooms
E ager to score the goal
A nd we are off
M an of the match!

Nat Bagnall (9)
Harriers Ground Primary School

Heartbroken

My boyfriend called the other night,
his voice echoes in my ear,
by the end of the call we'd broken up,
I shed many a tear.

I was full of self-pity,
my friends misunderstand,
I need a boy to hug at night,
a boy to hold my hand.

I was so broken-hearted,
my boyfriend had left me,
half of my heart had gone with him,
he was my life, you see.

But now I am quite over him,
I've met another guy,
his name is Ben, he's oh so sweet,
but also painfully shy!

Amelia Macmillan (10)
Harriers Ground Primary School

Anger

My fists are balling up,
My torso is tight.
A fire is roaring deep inside me.
I can see dark red.
There is a raging stallion in my belly,
Kicking and fighting to get out.
My palms start itching
And my fingers are slippery.
My teeth scratch against each other.
My mouth shapes angry words,
But with no noise.
My breath is cracked and dry
And will not come out easily.
I feel incorrectly made,
When I am angry.

Elizabeth Shelmerdine (9)
Kingham Primary School

Incorrectly Made?

'You're incorrectly made,' they say,
The boys and girls at school.
'You're incorrectly made,' they say,
'You really are a fool.'
They think I can't do things
That actually I can.
I should open up my wings -
Show them I'm a man;
I should soar up in the sky, way on high
And just tell them why they shouldn't make me cry.

They are a mean bunch,
Heavy chains and all,
Who say I'll hear a crunch from my fall
If they don't see my lunch money tomorrow at all.

'You're incorrectly made,' they say,
The boys and girls at school,
But I know better
For I am not a fool.
They shout their problems to me aloud
By picking on me and pulling up a crowd.
Why pick on me?
They could be incorrectly made,
Don't they see?
But it's not mine or their decision
So don't ask me . . .

Jonathan Shelmerdine (10)
Kingham Primary School

Happiness

Happiness feels like laughter.
Happiness is like children playing football.
Happiness tastes like ice cream.
Happiness looks like ice cream melting on a summer day.
Happiness reminds me of me skiing.

Ben Marsh (8)
Lewknor Primary School

Anger

Anger reminds me of the war.
It tastes like maggot pie
And smells of cow poo.
It looks like rotten bones
And it feels like slime on dungeon walls.
It sounds like explosions.

Will Rose (8)
Lewknor Primary School

Hunger

Hunger sounds like the sorrowful world without human beings.
Hunger tastes like a long dry desert in your mouth.
Hunger smells like the distant food that you can never reach.
Hunger feels like demons inside your stomach.
Hunger looks like skinny children rummaging in dustbins.
Hunger reminds me of a world without crops and animals.

Nicholas Greaves (9)
Lewknor Primary School

Darkness

Darkness looks like death and destruction.
Darkness sounds like screaming.
It tastes like a dagger in your neck.
It smells like flesh.
Darkness reminds me of death.
It feels like bullets hitting your head.

Hamish Bowie (8)
Lewknor Primary School

Fear

Fear sounds like someone screaming in your ear.
Fear feels like a wolf howling at the moon.
Fear looks like the world black as night.
Fear reminds me of a black apparition.
Fear tastes like a horrid sweet.
Fear smells like a rotten smell.

James Stoddart (10)
Lewknor Primary School

Happiness

Happiness sounds like carol-singers outside your doorstep.
Happiness feels like galloping across the sandy beach.
It looks like a couple coming out of the old white wedding church.
It reminds me of when I won a jumping competition on my
                                        strawberry roan pony, Harvey.
It tastes like strawberries covered in melted chocolate
With gooey marshmallows spread all over them.
It smells like beautiful red roses in a bouquet.

Rebecca Davies (8)
Lewknor Primary School

Hunger

It feels like a rat scratching away in your throat.
It looks like death from a glinting knife.
It smells like a dry world.
It tastes like dry earth.
It sounds like a dizzy ratty roar.
It reminds me of an itchy cockroach up my spine.

Daniel Lamb (9)
Lewknor Primary School

Fear

Fear reminds me of dark maggots,
Cockroaches in the night when they crawl around in bed.
Fear feels like vast creepy-crawlies in the dark, slimy, deep well
With furry rats with smelly cheese.
Fear smells like rotten apples and rat droppings.
Fear tastes like raw spiders and cold slugs.
Fear sounds like old rock music - very creepy.

Laura Swain (8)
Lewknor Primary School

Fear

Fear sounds like mighty storms crashing in the wind,
It feels like apparitions murmuring in a deep dark dungeon.
Fear looks like damp, dead bodies lying on wet blood,
It reminds my heart of World War II.
Fear tastes like mouldy oranges rushing down my throat,
It smells like evil is approaching.

Ben McIntosh (8)
Lewknor Primary School

Love

It feels like you've just woken up in a world full of girls,
It tastes like a juicy red strawberry,
It sounds like two hearts crashing together,
It smells as good as a beautiful red rose,
It reminds me of a lovely warm bath,
It looks as good as a warming mug of cocoa.

Jack McIntosh (10)
Lewknor Primary School

Laughter

It sounds like my friend is making me laugh.
It makes me happy when somebody is really funny.
It feels like I'm having a fun day.
It feels like I'm having a wicked sleepover with my best friend.
It feels like I'm having fun at my friend's house
Watching a movie with my friend and having popcorn.
That's all the things that I like about laughter.

Holly Sutton (10)
Lewknor Primary School

Hate

The crashing of thunder, the pounding of rain,
Hate feels like all happiness has gone down the drain.
It tastes like boiling lava running down my neck,
It makes me feel like a total wreck.
Hate reminds me of wolves howling in the moonlight,
It reminds me of monsters that come out at night.
It smells like apples rotting in a bowl.
Hate looks like a big black hole.

Lucy Vaughan (9)
Lewknor Primary School

Fear

Fear is like cockroaches crawling up your spine,
Spiders hanging from the roof,
Maggots coming through the floor,
Crashing and crawling,
Bones on the floor.
The room smells like rotten green smoke
Making you choke.

Dominic James Savin (9)
Lewknor Primary School

Love

Love tastes like sweet strawberries soaked in hot melted chocolate.
Love smells like a bouquet of white roses
being held by the bridesmaids of the happy couple's wedding.
Love sounds like the violins playing for Romeo and Juliet
at the matinee of the midnight musical.
Love reminds me of a gleaming diamond engagement ring
in a red velvet box, being held by the man of everyone's dreams.
Love feels like Heaven and when you kiss
fireworks set off and nothing else matters!

Lily-May Anson (11)
Lewknor Primary School

Anger

When I've had an argument and I'm feeling hot with anger,
I take it out on my little sister and I bash her and I bang her.
Then I go up to my room and think it all over.
I think about how much I hate feeling anger.
How it feels like being plunged into a red-hot fire
With the flames growing around you getting higher and higher.
How it sounds like a blood-curdling scream
And it fills my body with boiling hot steam.
How it tastes like mud, it makes me want to
Fall down dead with a thud.
How it looks like a million people tearing at
Each other's deathly white skin,
How it reminds me of someone breaking their neck,
Their arm and their shin.
How it smells like blood dripping fresh from someone's neck.
Anger makes me feel like a total, total wreck.

Lyla Fibert (9)
Lewknor Primary School

Hunger

It feels like your tummy is empty.
It reminds you of having no food in your fridge.
It smells like cold empty dark places.
It tastes like chips and beans.
It sounds like rumbling in your tummy.

Deacon Ashworth (10)
Lewknor Primary School

Hate

Hate sounds like doors slamming and crashing in the wind,
It feels like you can't control yourself,
It looks like an enormous black hole sucking you in.
Hate reminds you of your enemy,
It tastes like a sea of souls.
Hate smells like the ash in a fireplace.

Charlotte Coles (9)
Lewknor Primary School

Anger

Anger sounds like somebody screaming in your ear.
Anger feels like all of the happiness is draining out of you.
Anger looks like a red-hot volcano.
Anger reminds me of somebody bullying me.
Anger tastes like demons going through my mind.
Anger smells like mouldy food and seaweed.

Megan Hawkes (10)
Lewknor Primary School

Love

Love is the most beautiful thing in the world,
Love smells like rich and red strawberries growing
On a hot summer's day,
Love sounds like church bells ringing
On a hot summer's day,
Love reminds you of beautiful red hearts
With red roses falling gently on you
On a hot summer's day,
Love tastes like rich strawberries
Dipped in a soothing chocolate fountain
On a hot summer's day,
Love feels like cuddling a red and soft heart pillow
On a hot summer's day,
Love looks like a man and woman getting married
On a hot summer's day!

Gemma Sutton (8)
Lewknor Primary School

Darkness

Darkness sounds like a big storm thrashing
And crashing outside your door.
Darkness feels like a cold, dark, wet dungeon.
Darkness looks like a black hole waiting for your doom.
Darkness reminds me of walking in a deep, dark, haunted dungeon
On Hallowe'en night.
Darkness tastes of mouldy apples and soft bananas.
Darkness smells like a corpse lying in front of you.

Amy Miles (11)
Lewknor Primary School

Hate

Hate sounds like a fierce thing ringing through my ears.
It feels like I've fallen in a dull black hole.
It looks like a dry swimming pool.
It reminds me of being bullied.
It tastes of rotten apples.
It smells of soot.

Georgia Rose Morrow (8)
Lewknor Primary School

Love

Love sounds like church bells ringing on a summer's day.
Love feels like two people having a baby.
Love looks like a red rose smelling like lovely perfume.
Love reminds me of a romantic walk to the park in the moonlight.
Love tastes like melted chocolate on your lips.
Love smells like the richest perfume in the world.

Adam Muttitt (11)
Lewknor Primary School

Happiness

Happiness reminds me of being at home
relaxing in front of the evening's fire.
To me happiness looks like a meadow
full of lovely flowers of all kinds.
When I am happy I hear birds singing in the early morn.
Rocking side to side on a boat at sea
in a hot country makes me feel happy.
I think happiness smells like a roast dinner
followed by a lush apple crumble with ice cream on Sunday.
Happiness tastes to me like chocolate covered strawberries,
under an apple tree in the shade on a hot summer's day.
Those are all the things I feel like when I am happy!

Elisabeth J Gowens (10)
Lewknor Primary School

Anger!

Anger sounds like howling werewolves at night
When the full moon arrives.

Anger feels like a volcano erupting
And when the lava reaches you it burns you to death.

Anger looks like a blazing fire and screams from the girls
That are getting burnt, they are never heard again.

Anger reminds me of people being murdered
And having sharp needles being stabbed in you.

Anger tastes like mouldy sour milk
That's been kept out for 100 years.

Anger smells like poison that has been mixed up
With bogies and dead people.

Isabella Carroll (9)
Lewknor Primary School

Six Years Of My Life

War is like Hell,
I hate it so much,
When it comes to the time I cannot understand why.
I smell the smoke pouring into the night sky.
The sirens start singing with flickers of flames
From the burning fire in the gaze.

Bombs start dropping with crashes and bangs,
I feel the blood rushing through me like there's no care in the world.
I see women running, children screaming and worst of all,
Children and adults lying on the ground without a movement.

And then the houses break and nothing can be done.
I hear the screaming and trampling with bombs all around
And all I do now is fall to the ground.

Hollie Harrison (10)
Manor Primary School

Battleground

The thundering explosions on the ground,
Bullets firing all around.
Poke your head out,
Then you won't even have time to shout.
The eerie sound of a shell slicing through the air
Like a knife through butter.

Nightfall, not a sound to be heard,
Not even a bird.
Trying to get some sleep,
Still not a peep.
Suddenly a dense smoke as dark as Hell
Engulfs everyone.

Clearing the slimy corpses from the day before,
Broken bones and horrific gore.
Craters seemingly as deep as a well,
Oh what will stop this awful hell?
The devastation seems as endless as
The universe itself.

Gabriel Naughton (11)
Manor Primary School

Dreadful School

When I wake up and realise it's school,
I try to be ill but my mum's not fooled.
I heave my heavy bones and drag myself downstairs
And then I pull my sister's hair, 'Oww that's not fair!'

I run to school because I'm late,
Oh no I'm being taught by a teacher I hate.
The teacher asks me to stay behind,
I think I'm gonna lose my mind.
It's time for ICT and I blow the PC up deliberately.

My mum's not happy when she's phoned up
Then she finds out she owes them a million bucks!
Then I found out that school totally sucks.

Rosie Darby (10)
Manor Primary School

Hitler

Most people think I'm bad,
Others just think I'm sad.

I hate the sound of gunshots,
But my people still love me a lot.

I'm starting to get older,
My best mate died a soldier.

I don't want them to suffer,
I never was much of a peace lover.

I'll save my wife, myself and my dog,
All I can see is black and grey fog.

Fráe Mary Elford Bennett (11)
Manor Primary School

Dying

I never thought it would ever happen,
The horrifying experience of my bones crackin',
With death coming on the way,
I thought I'd better say,
Goodbye!

You've been there when I needed you the most
And now I'm here dying on the coast,
Don't forget me wherever you may go,
You'll always be in my heart's content flow.

So I say goodbye,
As I cry into the night,
You'll always be with me wherever I go,
I'll be dead by the next morning's crow.

Jamie Blair (11)
Manor Primary School

The Blitz

The pain and sorrow of a dying heart,
bleeds with blood.

I can smell smoke and rotting bodies,
like mouldy cheese in the mud.

Everyone can taste bitter blood and pain,
like old milk pouring in my mouth.

We can all hear the air raid sirens,
like a choking cat.

I can see planes, dirt, bodies and tears,
like a funeral in the cold.

Alice Strange (11)
Manor Primary School

In The War

The cries and yelps of people being bitten by death,
Buried with others with this spreading plague.
The day moves on, more and more die,
Some in trucks, some on foot, some in planes.
Bombs falling on friends and foe,
The stench of rotting bodies and fire.
The feel of mud on feet and the sound of gunshots
Deafens the day.

Elizabeth Alcock (10)
Manor Primary School

When I Die

When I die remember me but don't remember the war.
I may have been a bad soldier, I may have been good,
But either way I fought for my country
And risked my life for you.

Through all the bombs and gunshots I could have been killed
But the only thing stopping me from wanting to be
Was my wife and my daughter.

For every friend I had has now been put in a grave
And my family at home are all suffering as well.

Ruby Livesey (10)
Manor Primary School

It's My Fault!

As we went to war,
He comforted me all the way,
We were best friends but now he's gone,
It's my fault.

When he got blown up,
I could not believe it,
Those cruel Germans,
It was my fault.

He was a true hero,
There was no doubt about it,
A gunner no one would ever be,
It was my fault he died.

Jake Bristow (10)
Manor Primary School

The Seasons

In the spring the flowers bloom,
The birds are singing too,
Little lambs are prancing around,
With nothing much to do.

In the summer the sun is warm,
Everybody is away on holiday,
Lying on the beach to get a tan,
It is so hot you will need to use a fan.

In the autumn the leaves are falling,
And turning different colours,
Hallowe'en is coming soon,
Outside it's dark with the glowing moon.

In the winter it starts to get cold,
Christmas is here at last,
Then the snow falls from the sky,
With white snowflakes all on the grass.

Fern Holliday (11)
Manor Primary School

Do You Know Me?

I sway back and forth,
As the wind hits my top,
But under my shelter,
Live the creatures I take care of.

They come in all shapes and sizes,
But I don't care,
Their world is in me,
I have the key to let them in.

Above me is laughter and play,
The sun cools me down,
My waves hit rock bottom,
As I swish across the sand.

White horses live in me,
Even though I'm blue,
I go on for miles and miles
And touch the bottom of the Earth.

My land is not flat,
But really bumpy,
I go up and down,
As I run left and right.

When a day comes to an end,
I'm still shining bright,
With my wonderful world,
What am I?

Katie Payne (11)
Manor Primary School

Waiting For Peace

I'm waiting now waiting for the end.
Every minute seems like an hour.
All I hear are sniper shots.
This dugout I'm in seems so low.
Mud and grass is all I can see.
Dead men all around me.
I know I'll be one of them soon.

Lewis Miltenberger (11)
Manor Primary School

Air Raid

The siren wails like a hungry baby,
It wakes me up in the night,
All I can think is in the morning,
London will be a terrible sight.

I run down the stairs with my mum and my sister
And dive under the nearest chair,
Why did they have to bomb London?
It really isn't fair.

We run down the garden
And into the shelter,
While the planes roar above,
While the bombs drop and pelter.

A plane drops a bomb
And blows our shelter into smithereens,
We have to quickly run out,
Into the terrible scenes.

The all clear sirens go off,
What a relief,
We've survived the night,
By the skin of our teeth.

Sam Keogh (10)
Manor Primary School

Concentration Camps

Here in this concentration camp,
Death is drawing near.
And every day we have a fear,
That it may be our last day on Earth.

But ho ho! We are saved,
The tunnel is dug for our freedom.
We live our last minutes of boredom,
And we're all cramped into a hut.

We plan the finer details,
And file underground.
The joy is piled on in mounds,
As we scuttle to our buddies.

Robert Pocock (11)
Manor Primary School

Dogs Are . . .

Dogs are a tree that's had a trim,
Dogs are a pot full right to the brim.

Dogs are a skunk that's lifted its tail,
Dogs are a sky full of freezing hail.

Dogs are a star high up in the sky,
Dogs are a man rolling his eyes.

Dogs are a moon in a bright space,
Dogs are a hare in a race.

Dogs are all the good things in life.

Annie Royal (10)
Manor Primary School

Here In The Trenches

Here in the trenches we lie waiting.
Just waiting.
Then the cry of war rings out over no-man's-land.
The shrapnel's everywhere
Guns firing.
Dead lie there, still as stone,
Never to see the light of day again.

Others are on bloodstained stretchers, hoping,
Praying, that one day they will see the faces of their
                                                  loved ones again.

A body hanging from the barbed wire, hand pointing skywards.
'That's where I want to be.'

Christopher Dalley (10)
Manor Primary School

Victory

The yelling, the screaming, where has it gone?
I feel I could drop a pin on the ground,
Why can I not hear what is going on?

I can hear something in the distance, it's people,
But it's not bad it's a sound of happiness.

Then I see people come over the hill
My heart takes the badness away and I'm full of joy.

I smell no smoke or rotting dead,
We have all defeated Hell except the ones who have been
                                                        taken by the evil.

When I go home, I shall kiss my wife
And then I will know how lucky I am to be one who has stayed alive.

Olivia Jones (10)
Manor Primary School

Love

Love is gold,
It smells like a candle burning.
Love tastes sweet and jolly,
It sounds like a sigh of gladness,
It feels soft and comfortable.
Love lives in the middle of your heart.

Matthew Allison (10)
Marcham Primary School

Anger

Anger is blood-red,
It smells like a hot piece of metal melting.
Anger tastes sour and sharp,
It sounds like a hand going down a blackboard,
It feels cold and bitter.
Anger lives in the heart of a monster.

Robin Butt (10)
Marcham Primary School

War

War is ruby-red,
It smells like blood dripping from a body.
War tastes sad and sour,
It sounds like a roaring monster,
It feels rough and hard.
War is a harsh thing.

Robert Gresham (9)
Marcham Primary School

Rainbow

A rainbow is all colours that grab your eye,
It smells of all your favourite perfume,
It tastes of a mountain of ice cream,
The sound of the rainbow is saying,
Believe in yourself.
It's so cuddly and it lives in your imagination.

Ben Ireson (9)
Marcham Primary School

Hate

Hate is illuminated,
It smells like frozen snail slime.
Hate tastes like mouldy porridge on a Sunday morning,
It sounds like a heartbeat suddenly going dead,
It feels like nails going down a blackboard.
Hate lives in a dark old cave.

Jamie Saulter (10)
Marcham Primary School

Despair

Despair is azure,
It smells like rotting fish.
Despair tastes squashed and slimy,
It sounds like someone screaming,
It feels hot and stinging.
Despair lives in the heart of the forests of time.

Harriet Scott (9)
Marcham Primary School

Happiness

Happiness is colourful,
It smells like perfume,
It tastes like candyfloss,
It sounds like bubble and pop,
It feels like a chinchilla,
It lives inside me!

George Newman (10)
Marcham Primary School

Anger

Anger is rouge,
It smells like boiling irons seething.
Anger tastes burnt and flaring,
It sounds like teeth rubbing together,
It feels hard and razor-like.
Anger lives in the heart of a volcano.

Kieran Belcher (8)
Marcham Primary School

Fear

Fear is indigo,
It smells like smoke.
Fear tastes like blood,
It sounds like a rattlesnake.
Fear lives under the sea.

Aleisha Fraser (9)
Marcham Primary School

Love

Love is a ruby,
It smells like a rose,
It tastes like strawberries,
It feels like Heaven.
Love is in your heart.

Sarah Tierney (8)
Marcham Primary School

Anger

Anger is damson,
It sounds like a blistering iron flaring,
It tastes burnt and pungent,
It sounds like teeth grating together,
It feels dense and razor-sharp.
Anger lives in the heart of a volcano.

Louis Jackson (8)
Marcham Primary School

Whale

There was a blue
Whale which flew
Through the sea, it was long
And humming a song.

It was fast
And loved chewing a mast
It was fat
Like a greedy rat.

It was round
And weighed a pound
The whale
Drank a pail
Then it swam away
In dismay.

Freddie O'Donald (9)
Moulsford Preparatory School

The Wood

The wood is a great place to be,
I like to climb a tall strong tree.
Once I finally get to the top
I have a feeling that I should stop.

Down on the ground,
The dog runs around.
He runs at the speed
Of a greyhound.

Unlike a small deer's horns
There are tiny prickly thorns.
Up on the hill I tell you no lies,
There are lots of butterflies.

Freddie Carr (9)
Moulsford Preparatory School

My Chicken Is . . .

She's as good as gold,
She's really bold,
And you will often see,
Her sitting on my knee.

She's had a lucky escape from a hungry fox,
By keeping quiet in the laying box.
Plump as a cushion with pencil legs,
She quietly lays us golden eggs.

With a turn of her head her curious eye
Spots tasty morsels coming by.
Cheese and raisins and porridge make her fuss,
We're so glad she lives with us.

Tristan Benfield (9)
Moulsford Preparatory School

Jack Russell

I have a dog
Who is a Jack Russell,
She causes a lot of
Hustle and bustle.

She eats a lot,
And is really fat,
She is always chasing
Next-door's cat.

She is fluffy
And snowy white,
Last night she got into
A terrible fight.

She is gorgeous,
Chocolate-brown,
She will sometimes give
A horrible frown.

Ed Howlett (9)
Moulsford Preparatory School

Hair

Some hairstyles are weird,
Some are even feared.
Some are short and groovy,
Others are long and smoothy!

Hair comes in all different shades,
You can change the colour if you have paid.
From white to black to grey,
You can dye it all 3 in one day.

Boys at this school have theirs short,
It's what the teachers have taught!

George Buckley (9)
Moulsford Preparatory School

Drama

When I go to drama on a Saturday morning,
I have to get up early and often find I'm yawning.
We are nearly done with 'James and the Giant Peach',
It's coming up, it's coming up, as James I have to reach,
Coz I am James, James with the peach.

The peach is made from a bright spotlight,
And with the help of seagulls, it dances through the night!
The director is called Hector, and his brother is called Dexter.
I always have good fun, like I say, we're almost done.

Jordy Williams (10)
Moulsford Preparatory School

The Elephant

The elephant is exciting,
The elephant is inviting,
The elephant is a lovely creature,
The elephant has a brilliant feature.

The elephant is very strong,
The elephant has a nice song,
The elephant has big ears,
The elephant can have fears.

The elephant has a big trunk,
The elephant is a big hunk,
The elephant is very massive,
The elephant is quite passive.

And that is why I like the elephant!

Max Hearnden (9)
Moulsford Preparatory School

Black

Black is darkness, black is mist,
Black is night, black is hiss,
Black is weary, black is damp,
And as we know black is *scary!*

Black is a cat,
Black is a panther, black is a bat,
Black is stormy, black is school,
Black is a crow, black is a *fool!*

Mike Garside (9)
Moulsford Preparatory School

Football Crazy

I love football, defence is my position,
I often give the strikers concussion,
Whack, crack, smack.
I love football,
Scoring goals,
My favourite player is Paul Scholes,
Whack, crack, smack.
I love football,
Our kit is red,
I play number nine,
That number will always be mine,
Whack, crack, smack.

Conor Anderson (9)
Moulsford Preparatory School

Skateboarding

Skateboarding is such fun,
Sometimes you need to run.
Sometimes there are big bumps,
They are very good for jumps.

Skateboarding is so cool,
But beware it's easy to fall.
Wear a helmet on your head,
Or you may well end up dead.

Alex Butt (9)
Moulsford Preparatory School

Curiosity

There is the smell of fear in the air,
Looking round the corner, is anything there?
Just about to open the door,
Thinking, *is there anything more?*
There's something there, it's just the cat
And there's nothing else, but what is that?
It's just my dear boxer dog,
How silly of me, thinking it's a hog.
Turning on the cooker and
Would it really burn my hand?
If I went out in the dark,
Would people scare me for a lark?
Look out the window it is night,
And I got a terrible fright.
When I sat watching TV
Something really came to me,
Well, nothing happened today,
The smell of fear has gone away.

Daniel Watts (10)
Moulsford Preparatory School

What A Game!

The teams start,
Beckham gets a card,
Crespo gets a goal!
He celebrates with the roll,
And smiles at Joe Cole.

Rooney chips onto the post,
Ooohhh man, how close!
Seconds later in the net,
Argentina start to sweat,
A cross put in.

Samuel gets it in,
Cross from Gerrard,
Owen scores a goal and celebrates with the flagpole,
He hugs Ashley Cole,
One minute left.

It's a draw, but wait,
Owen far post,
The whistle goes,
Riquelme makes a deep blow,
Argentina look low.

William Ottosson (10)
Moulsford Preparatory School

Churches

Churches are big,
Churches are small,
We also pray in churches.

Churches are generous,
Churches are good,
And churches are extremely peaceful.

We're christened in churches,
We're married in churches,
And churches are the best way to talk to God.

Henry Graham (10)
Moulsford Preparatory School

Gold

The gleaming gold was extremely cold,
It was glimmering and glossy and waiting to be sold,
Shining and shimmering the man was told,
This precious necklace was outstandingly bold.

Alex Harmer (11)
Moulsford Preparatory School

Night On The Beach

The sun was set,
The sea was wet,
This is somewhere I've never been,
The sea was looking a murky green.

Is this the way?
Look there's somewhere to play,
We should not go there,
Oh well, I don't care.

Now the sea is blue,
Like it was brand new,
It was cool,
Waves bouncing like a ball.

You could hear the sea in your ear,
It sounded like a cheer,
It was nearly night,
I could see the moonlight.

At one o'clock,
I could hear the sound of tick-tock,
The sea made no noise,
My dog and me, us boys.

Toby Stoddart (11)
Moulsford Preparatory School

The 7.40 Paddington Express

It stops at stations big and small,
It tumbles past the big red wall,
It whistles and hoots at passing trains,
And criss-crosses the country lanes.

It runs on the rails front or back,
It races through tunnels small and black,
It screeches on rails strong and stout,
And that's what this poem is all about.

Henry Ellis (10)
Moulsford Preparatory School

Mountain Biking

On a hot summer's day the sunlight beams,
On my mountain bike everything is great or so it seems.
As you glide over a gigantic jump,
Oh no, I hit my toe on a big stump.

I hit hard on the muddy ground,
'Ow!' I howl like a hound,
All my friends come over in a run,
They all shout, 'Was that crash super fun?'

Karl Simmons (11)
Moulsford Preparatory School

School

I'm going through the gate,
I think I am late,
School is such a bore,
What is four plus four?

I'm off to history,
I really need a wee,
I should be at French,
But I'm sitting on a bench.

A boy gets kicked in games,
Guess who the teacher blames?
I kick a ball at his face,
But hit a different place.

He then gets really mad,
He says that I was bad,
He hangs me on a rack,
And *crack* goes my back.

And now I see my mum,
She's seen me sucking my thumb,
I'm getting in the car,
With a big chocolate bar!

Jack Maple (10)
Moulsford Preparatory School

Night Cats

Down in the dark gloomy night
With the stars shining light
And the moon shining bright
Down walks the cats of delight
Walk the wonderful street-lit night
All boys chasing their only delight
Down in the wonderful street-lit night.

Trevor Warner (10)
Moulsford Preparatory School

The Dark Wood

I could feel the wind on my ears,
I was fighting the battle against my fears.
The leaves were crunching against my shoes,
It was nothing like a Caribbean cruise.

The fog has dropped, the night fell,
The cold was feeling a lot like Hell.
I can't see anything straight ahead,
All I want is to get to bed.

The house next door, its lights are on,
All the fear is finally gone.
I was running now,
The cold has gone, and I don't know how.

There it is, the light of my house,
The wood was in pieces, because of a louse.
I was into the door,
Feeling the warmth of the underfloor.

Toby Worrall Thompson (10)
Moulsford Preparatory School

The Barracuda

One hot, sunny day under the Australian sun,
A barracuda came out to have some fun.
He was going to have fun on that hot summer's day.

He was swimming on that hot summer's day
And he came across his frightened prey,
That prey never remembered that hot summer's day.

As the barracuda is chomping away,
He now becomes a type of prey,
He may never remember that hot summer's day.

Behind him saw a large school of cray,
Little barracuda, he started to run away,
Chomp! He left the whole world on that hot summer's day.

Patrick Lawson Statham (10)
Moulsford Preparatory School

Music

Music has so many instruments,
It is played by ladies and gents.

There are writers like Beethoven and Robbie Williams,
They've been selling CDs by the millions.

Some is classical, some is funk,
Some is just a pile of junk.

Some get very famous and very rich,
Some screw up and go down in the ditch.

Some rock bands go on tour,
The singer's voice becomes very sore.

Music is very worthwhile,
The sound sometimes makes you smile.

Handel made firework music for folk,
The Catherine wheels went up in smoke.

In the end music is fantastic,
In a show conductors go elastic.

Music is something I'm passionate about,
If you don't like it I'll give you a clout.

Ben West (10)
Moulsford Preparatory School

Jemima

Crumpled and hot,
In her cot,
Awake to start the day.

A bottle of milk,
Brush her hair like silk,
She chuckles to herself,
Like a little elf.

Change her nappy,
To make her happy,
Breakfast on her face,
And every other place.

Tottering like a penguin,
On her tiny feet,
My cousin Jemima,
Isn't she sweet.

Leo Wood (10)
Moulsford Preparatory School

In The Trenches

In the trenches it is dark and dank
The soldiers are the backbone of their country
They fight for their queen and their pride
As they look into the deep dark sky
They come in and out of sleep dreaming of England.

As they look out through the mist and smoke at the enemy
They wish that they could live all together in harmony
As they jump and move forward
They are scared, scared for their lives
Then a shell explodes, one man falls as they all sigh
And think what it would be like in the green pastures of England.

Their family at home always pray for their brave people
Back on the battlefield the men are running
The men on the ground cry out with blood-curdling screams
As their friends and comrades run by
The allies run into the Germans thinking only of their family . . .
And England.

The poppies grow out of control as they fight to gain sun
As the blood-red colour of them blinds modern people
But the men who have fought are not forgotten
Many are remembered by modern people today
In a very modern England.

Tom Godfrey (10)
Moulsford Preparatory School

The Menu

'Rotten ham with mouldy bread,
Beetle blood with hedgehog's head,
Fat tree-frog's slime.' Then I said,
'What else is on the menu?'

'Snotty nose stuffed with earwax,
Fondue of fishes' broken backs.'
I stopped the waiter in his tracks,
'What else is on the menu?'

'Hazel pig's eyes in a soap bar,
Mixed-up ketchup with tartar,
Whilst the waiters perform on guitars!'
'What else is on the menu?'

'Moss and bark scraped from a dead tree,
Golden sand stolen from the Irish Sea.'
He panted, he was puffed out, I could see.
'What else is on the menu?'

'Intestine soup with liver fudge,
A bruised, bloody dog with a kick and a nudge.'
I think he was holding an angry grudge.
'That's what's on the menu!'

Toby Marlow (11)
Moulsford Preparatory School

Winter

Winter is frosty and freezing in the moonlight,
It shines on the snow and it is pure white.
Sparkles of snow drop down upon us.
In the moonlight it shines with a gorgeous light on the snow.
Animals are hibernating in the freezing winter snow.
Hailstones hit the floor with a crash,
While everything is peaceful for the night.
The animals are getting ready for the summer
Collecting acorns in the freezing winter of death.
It's getting colder and colder until it's as rough as a hurricane.

James Fotherby (8)
Moulsford Preparatory School

A Knight's Tale

A long time ago, far, far away,
There sat a dragon on a dreary day,
He had a stripy back and a spiky tail,
The rain outside was turning to hail.

Soon a very brave knight came,
Who thought the dragon could be tame,
Soon his tired horse went lame,
He had to wait till the dragon came.

He saw the dragon as it came silently in,
Its glistening scales were like shiny nails on its skin,
The dragon's teeth were slimy and bared,
This made him very, very scared.

So he decided the dragon dead would be best,
Then ran at the dragon and speared it in the chest,
The dragon turned and flew away,
And the knight had a very victorious day!

Hamish Veitch (8)
Moulsford Preparatory School

My Dog

I have a dog called Gunner,
He is an amazing runner.
He runs round and round
And never sits down
Until he crashes to the ground.

Joe Ellis (8)
Moulsford Preparatory School

Lizard Hunting

Lizard hunting on a humid day,
At the Bahia Principe.
Looking in the grey stone wall,
I couldn't see anything at all.

Getting angry, getting mad,
I wanted a lizard really bad.
But watching me with big black eyes,
It was a lizard, oh what a surprise!

I stood there motionless for a while,
On my face was a great big smile.
I lunged forward quick as a flash,
I landed with an enormous crash.

In my hand the lizard stood,
I was feeling really good,
Until I realised he had no tail,
It made my face go kind of pale.

Ollie Butt (11)
Moulsford Preparatory School

Spring

The long spring grass came up to my knees,
Cascading in the morning breeze.

Beyond field mice there lay a stream,
The sunlight made the water gleam.

I was nearly there, not long now,
Only a field with a lonely cow.

Then I came to the end of the field,
The dazzling light made my eyes need a shield.

I've often tried but try as I might,
I cannot bear this amazing sight.

The falling water didn't stop,
Until the bottom of the sheer drop.

Standing from this amazing height,
I see Niagara Falls, gleaming bright.

Henry Binning (11)
Moulsford Preparatory School

The Bloody War

The soldiers are brave I say,
Through the day
And through the night,
All the time they stand and fight,
Throughout the bloody war.

They hardly get any sleep,
The deaths of friends make them weep,
Their loving family stay at home,
As all the soldiers continue to roam,
Throughout the bloody war.

Gunshots here and there,
People are dying everywhere,
Explosions killing hundreds of men,
Each bomb killing ten,
Throughout the bloody war.

James Bywater (11)
Moulsford Preparatory School

Dancing With Dolphins

I've dreamed to swim with the dolphins
Who swim in the ocean blue
And this very Christmas
My greatest wish came true.

The most beautiful morning ever
The sun shining so bright
I see these amazing figures
And I can't believe my sight.

Quickly to the water
With these mammals so near
Their squealing and their laughter
Is the only sound I hear.

Soon it is all over
The dolphins have swum away
All that's left is a memory
Of that very special day.

Jacob Simons (11)
Moulsford Preparatory School

A Scare At Sea

One beautiful sunny day,
On the southern coast of Spain
We travelled down to the sandy beach,
With no sight of the rain.

I hopped into my boat,
My dad had heaved it out,
But when I sat on the bumpy sea,
I started to scream and shout.

The wave was galloping down
To the sandy shore,
As it was coming nearer
I shouted more and more.

The wave had flipped me over
Into the salty sea,
I was gasping round for air,
(And I was only three).

My dad had come to save me,
Swimming more and more,
Eventually he had done it!
And dragged me safe to shore.

David Wheatley (11)
Moulsford Preparatory School

Tsunami

The first day of the summer holidays,
Is always the best,
Like going to a playful beach,
To get a little rest.

The sun was gazing over the sea,
Bright as a bright white light,
So I went to the beautiful water,
And I saw an amazing sight.

A mammoth wave,
So amazing,
The white horses sprinting,
As the heat still blazing.

The wave was coming so fast,
That I could hardly see it coming,
While the people behind me were shouting,
Screaming and running.

I got my surfboard ready,
The wave was about to come,
As I looked behind me,
My adventure with the wave had begun.

I was underwater now,
I hit something solid,
The wave was going so fast,
My hand and the metal collided.

The wave was finally over,
I hope that my home is alright,
Now I shall always remember,
That big and horrible fright.

Phin Leslau (10)
Moulsford Preparatory School

A Day In The Austrian Alps

The glistening white snow in the Austrian Alps,
The most beautiful sight without a doubt,
The powdery snow blowing around,
All of the skiers racing down.

The snow lay in front of me one metre deep,
Lying there in one enormous heap,
The temptation to dive in it was far too strong,
I had waited for this moment for far too long.

As I was leaping through the air,
I knew that this was too big of a dare,
I landed headfirst in the snow,
I called frantically to my best friend Joe.

My dad rushed over to heave me out,
As he had heard my desperate shouts,
He pulled me up onto my feet,
I was pretty shaken so I took a seat.

I was extremely scared I must say,
But I will never forget that beautiful day,
The dazzling snow, the twinkling sun,
Never in my life will I have so much fun.

Sam Lerche-Thomsen (10)
Moulsford Preparatory School

The Scrum

'Crouch!'
The shout of the referee
Begins to deafen me.
Anticipation makes my heartbeat faster
Knowing what will come after.

'Touch!'
The feel of the opposition's shirt
Hot with sweat and grimy with dirt.
My boots reach about for a good firm hold
In the slimy ground, I must be bold.

'Pause!'
The stench of earth and sweat combine
Into one strong smell that would rival a mine.
It intoxicates the body, warming it up against the cold
In a moment of quiet waiting to be told . . .

'Engage!'
Pain sears through my body as head meets shoulder
The weight of the opposition as strong as a boulder.
The crowd shouts so loud there's a fantastic din
What will we do if we cannot win?

Louis Allen (11)
Moulsford Preparatory School

Paradise

An island of paradise surrounded by deep blue,
The dazzling sunshine and beautiful view.
A glistening sun across crystal clear sea,
With colourful fish of every variety.

The rainforest, so lush and green,
With lots of creatures to be seen.
Exotic birds and monkeys too,
Of beautiful colours red, green and blue.

Midnight sky full of light
With twinkling stars which are so bright.
Moonlight glistens on the sea,
Provides a path for boats to see.

William Flindall (11)
Moulsford Preparatory School

Moulsford Prep School

Moulsford Prep is the best,
It is better than the rest,
My favourite teacher is Mr Murray,
He is never in any hurry.

He is so calm and cool,
But he hates football,
My favourite lesson is ICT,
This is taught by Docy B.

So now you know about my school,
You will know that it is very cool.

George Carr (11)
Moulsford Preparatory School

Magical Colours

Shiny like a glistening pearl,
Gleaming into a clean bright whirl,
Moving swiftly through the night,
The silver moon came creeping by,
Glistening and sparkling in the cold dark night,
The moonbeams tiptoe quietly by,
Lighting up all around,
The crispy, crunchy iced frosty ground.
The silver moon and its diamonds I have found.

Charlie Mansfield (11)
Moulsford Preparatory School

Slippery Lines

As I ski down beautiful mountains,
The powder behind me splashes like a fountain.
Powder is best!
It gives you zest!

The wind flies through my hair,
I would go faster . . . do I dare?
I hit a mogul; bump and grind,
All of a sudden I am stuck on my behind!

I am down, my legs are shaking,
My tired mind is almost breaking,
So I head down to the town,
Ready to snuggle in my eiderdown!

March Showering Russell (10)
Moulsford Preparatory School

My Cat

My cat is very old,
She does not like the cold.
She curls up on a chair,
And spends the whole day there.
But when she sees the sun,
She likes to have some fun.
And when she sees the rain,
She comes back in again.

My cat is very cheeky,
And always very sleepy.
She curls up on a bed,
And rests her sleepy head.
My cat loves to sleep,
And she loves to leap.

Jonathan Deacon (10)
Moulsford Preparatory School

Red

Red is the colour of traffic lights,
Red is the colour of mosquito bites,
Red is the colour of Hitler's army,
Red is the colour of some salami,
Red is the colour of a fingertip,
Red is the colour of a Man U strip.

I like red because it's cool,
It is the opposite of a swimming pool.

Hugh Barklem (10)
Moulsford Preparatory School

Subjects

History is a mystery.
Religious studies make you buddies.
Science explains an appliance.
French means you need to clench.
Maths is a way of adding up paths.
Art is where you make a chart.
Lunch is where you munch.
English is how you learn words like 'distinguish'.
Tables is where I am able.
IT is when we work for Doctor B.

JJ Sermon (8)
Moulsford Preparatory School

Making Up

There was Tom punching,
There was Dot hunching,
There was Tom kicking,
There was Dot nicking,
There was Tom biting,
There was Dot fighting,
There was Tom slapping,
There was Dot clapping.
'But stop!' said Sir,
'Don't pick on her!'
There was Tom looking sheepish
And wishing he had been
Kissing Dot instead!
There was Dot turning a deepish
Shade of red!

Rupert Boddington (10)
Moulsford Preparatory School

Charlie's Adventure

There sat Charlie, pulling a tablecloth,
When *smash*! Charlie broke a plate.
There sat Charlie, being punished away,
When, 'Out!' was heard.

There sat Charlie, asleep in his dog kennel,
When *ping!* Charlie started dreaming.
There sat Charlie, thinking what he had done,
There sat Charlie, thinking where he belonged.

There sat Charlie, deciding to go,
To go and find where he belonged.
There sat Charlie, walking down the street,
There sat Charlie, thinking about meat.

There sat Charlie, watching the train arrive,
There sat Charlie, hopping on board.
There sat Charlie, hoping he would arrive,
Where he belonged.

Thinking hard and thinking deep,
Charlie was thinking where.
The train arrived, and it just wasn't the place,
Charlie took a taxi to the countryside.

There sat Charlie, chasing cats and birds,
There sat Charlie, having so much fun.
Food and drink, were what he found,
Even some sweets on the ground.

By night, he found it hard and cold,
He felt like a bit of mould.
There sat Charlie, walking in the quietness,
There sat Charlie, walking into the darkness.
While he was walking, he whined one sentence to himself,
'There's no place like home.'

Henrik Cox (10)
Moulsford Preparatory School

Dogs

Dogs are fluffy,
Dogs are scruffy,
Dogs are hairy
And like to eat dairy,
Sometimes dogs are sad,
Sometimes dogs are barking mad,
Some are brown
And can act like a clown,
Some are white
And can give you a bite,
And some are black,
But they all like a snack.

Jamie Chapman (9)
Moulsford Preparatory School

Edinburgh Castle

As he walked up to Edinburgh Castle,
The only light was that of the street behind,
He could see the great black cannons peering out of the castle,
The great wooden gate was raised so high that no man could cross.

He could feel the cold hard stones beneath his leather shoes,
He could feel the light wind brush against his kilt,
His seal skin sporran was swaying from side to side in the wind,
His long dark brown hair was swaying in the wind.

His hand was clenched around his drawn dagger so tight,
His eyes were bloodshot with rage,
His hands were soaked with sweat,
His kilt was soaked with rain.

As he walked up to Edinburgh Castle,
He saw a musket raised over Edinburgh Castle,
He was shot in front of Edinburgh Castle,
There his cold hard body lay in front of Edinburgh Castle.

Nicholas Bryan (10)
Moulsford Preparatory School

Men At War

Two men stood in a warehouse
By a lake,
Not moving or talking
Knowing what was at stake.

Four men came in looking menacing and tough
Carrying knives and pistols and other dangerous stuff
But those men said nothing, nothing at all
Feeling quite nervous propped up against a wall.

Those two men were British and would come to any call
First they had family, now nothing at all.
When the Germans turned around the two men they said,
'Look now we can flee!'
When they got out they shouted, 'We're free, free,
I don't believe it free, free, free!'

That is the story of my great grandad Jamie,
He told his son, then his son, then, well he told me!

Harry Stott (10)
Moulsford Preparatory School

I Didn't Mean To Shout!

I didn't mean to shout,
I didn't mean to go out,
It just came over me, you know.

I didn't mean to slam the door,
I didn't mean to crack the floor,
It just came over me, you know.

I didn't mean to smash the glass,
I didn't mean to ruin the grass,
It just came over me, you know.

I didn't mean to lose the ball,
I didn't mean to break the wall,
It just came over me, you know.

I didn't mean to hurt the dog,
I didn't mean to kill the frog,
It just came over me, you know.

I didn't mean to rob the bank,
I didn't mean to kill Frank,
It just came over me, you know.

Tobias Whetton (9)
Moulsford Preparatory School

Two Tigers And A Mongrel

I had two tigers,
That lived on the attic floor,
And whenever they got hungry they always used to roar,
As rough as they sound,
They were quite cute and round,
They wouldn't hurt a fly,
Because they only like pie,
And when they got old I let them free,
And that's when they went on a killing spree,
After that they got shipped to the jungle,
And that's where they made friends with a mongrel,
And with that mongrel, they escaped from the jungle,
They didn't fancy the plane,
So they took the train,
On arrival at London,
They hitched a ride with Grundon,
It was a bit of a squeeze,
And it made them sneeze,
The driver looked round,
When he heard the sound,
But he didn't see the tigers,
Because he'd had too many ciders,
They jumped off at home,
Dodging the gnome,
They bounded the stairs,
While I was eating chocolate eclairs,
So now I have two tigers and a mongrel,
They come from the jungle.

Joe Tollet (10)
Moulsford Preparatory School

Bonfire Night

The bonfire is lit with burning torches,
And everybody goes to see it.
Its burning flames are really bright,
But if you go too near you'll have a fright.

The fireworks go flying up in the sky,
With lots of screeching and whistling.
All the sparks come down,
Which light up the people's faces on the ground.

William McDermott (9)
Moulsford Preparatory School

My Mum

Close your mouth my mum said to me,
As she took a long sip of tea,
Please eat your sprout,
Or at least your trout,
Please eat your peas,
Or at least your cheese.
I don't eat my peas or brocolli,
But hey, that's me!

Alex Andrews (10)
Moulsford Preparatory School

The Lizard And The Snake

There once was a lizard
Who ate a gizzard.
There once was a snake
Who ate a rake.
The snake slithered and slimed
And came up behind the lizard
And he ate the rest of the gizzard.
The lizard went mad
And did something bad,
Then the lizard ate the snake
And found the rest of the gizzard and the rake.

Benedict Rothschild (10)
Moulsford Preparatory School

Dubai

One hot summer's day in Dubai,
My holiday would soon fly by.
I strode down the bumpy road,
To and fro there I strode.

I slowly approached the big front door,
Then I suddenly slipped on the wet marble floor.
I got up to my feet once again
And saw a tall man who was 7ft 10.

I heaved myself into the gold-plated lift
If I could have some gold it would be a great gift
I went up to the top of the tall hotel,
And there in the restaurant great food they sell.

The restaurant was hanging over the sea
It was so high it really frightened me.
There were sailing boats and jet skis flying about below
They looked like lots of little dots and very fast they would go.

Sam Jones (10)
Moulsford Preparatory School

Horses

I saw a stallion striding in the sunlight,
I saw a Welsh cob whinnying in the wild,
I saw a Budyonny burning in the bright,
I saw a mother Caspian with calf child,
I saw a Lomud lying on the lawn,
I saw a Fresian fighting in the field,
I saw a Dale dancing in the dawn,
All the horses are revealed.

Rebecca Bonham (8)
Orchard Close, Sibford School

The Earth

The Earth is a big black spot
like on your face.
The Milky Way is a bottle of milk
as pale as your body.
Mars is a Mars bar
floating through space.
The moon is a cheese
ball bobbing up and down,
Because I am an astronaut
going home to the Earth.

Harry Little (9)
Orchard Close, Sibford School

Tractors

T ractors are big and powerful,
R oaming around the fields.
A lone with nature but
C arrying an anxious machine.
T urning the soft soil over and over again,
O verhead all the birds are singing.
R ound and round they fly,
S wooping down catching their prey.

James Paton (9)
Orchard Close, Sibford School

The Sea, Sun And Sky

No one knows the sea,
The beautiful, beautiful sea.
But I do with its elegant pure water
And its simple sloppy smile.

Everyone knows the sun,
The boiling, boiling sun.
It's so hot it could
Boil you to death.
Beware of it, it's immense and powerful
And also has mega rays.

Everyone knows the sky,
The wonderful, wonderful sky,
But why so high?
Oh why is the sky so high?
Oh why is the sky so high?

Jack Robins (9)
Orchard Close, Sibford School

Snow, Dirty Rain

S now is as white as paper,
N ow it falls from the sky,
O n the way we stick our tongues out and eat the snowflakes.
W hite snow is falling and falling.

D irt is slimy and wet,
I t is brown and slushy,
R unning slimy muck,
T ucked up in a big, fat blob.
Y uck, squish, squash.

R ain goes drip drop, drip drop.
A ir is wet and cold.
I nside it is dry and cosy,
N ot like the cold sharp rain.

Lali Slade (9)
Orchard Close, Sibford School

An Encounter With An Octopus

I walked into the horrible rusty shipwreck,
There was nothing to be seen.
I walked around on the creaky floors then I walked down
The stairs at the back of the cabin, there were layers
Of seaweed along the walls.
I bumped into a gigantic octopus, it didn't look happy to see me.
I saw piles of coins and bars of gold. I lunged towards the
Gold that looked very old, the octopus stopped me.
I swam away before I got hurt.
I reached the car and went home
And told everyone about the priceless gold.

Henry Wood (9)
Orchard Close, Sibford School

Exploring The Shipwreck

I plunge into the water
The deep, deep blue sea
Never beginning
Nor ending.

I can see a clump of something
Looming in the dark
I cannot work it out
It could be a log or a dense clump of weed
I think it is a shipwreck
Waiting to be seen.

I have swum nearer
Towards this strange sight
As if I am being pulled by an invisible string
Yes it is
A shipwreck indeed
Almost bigger than two double-decker buses.

I carry on searching
Round this massive site
In and out
All the scenes are new
Old cannon balls scattered between rivers of seaweed
Rusted and old -
Old human bones rotting away
This lost world is scary, interesting and fun.

Fish flicked around me like multicoloured darts
Bubbles of breath all around me
I have found a lake of coins - I pick them up and stare
Surprised to see they are not rusted.

I keep on searching, searching
But I don't know what for?

Charlotte Jayne Harrison (10)
Orchard Close, Sibford School

Shipwreck

I pounced into silvery, salty water
And plunged down below,
Pushing, pushing the seaweed.
Look! Look up ahead, look a shipwreck
All rusted up and gloomy smashing itself up.
I went inside and through the cabins up some steps
Into a room, a very dark room
Tucked under the slithering water under a cloth,
What was it?
A treasure chest that is what is hiding,
Hiding under a rotten cloth.
I stepped foot by foot over curling fish
Swimming to the enchanted thing.
It was all rusted, all rusted up
And *bang, bang* quick, I opened the magical thing.
Flicking it up such a wonderful sight,
Lots of lovely golden gold bars.
Lying, lying there shining in the glooming sunlight.
I packed them into a bag.
Bang, bang there it was again, what was the noise?
I packed the gold bars and turned to make a million,
Bang!
I was never seen again.

Jake Mayo (10)
Orchard Close, Sibford School

Under The Sea

I want to go under the sea
I bet there'll be lots of fish to see.
I saw a fish and a crab
And a man eating a kebab.
Wait, that's not a man,
Oh I wish I brought my cam'.
It's too big to be a man,
It's too big to be a van.
Wait, I think I know what it is,
Yes, it is a shipwreck.
I decided to go in
And I want those shiny things.
Wait, there's something in front of me
And it's bigger than a pea.
Oh, it's a massive octopus,
Get out of the way you octopussy
You really are an octowussy.
He looks kind of strong anyway
And I better not stay,
My oxygen is running out
So I better go up to shore.

Barney Cremin (10)
Orchard Close, Sibford School

Diving Down

I put on my heavy gear
And got ready to jump down into the huge pond.
I got down there and saw spotty, stripy and colourful fish.
I felt this strange slimy bush on my toes,
I went down further and saw something big,
I went closer and closer and saw a ship.
When I saw it I shivered from my head to my toe,
Then I felt braver and went inside,
It looked quite modern.
I went further, I saw fish and coral and more seaweed.

Inside lots of pictures of the past captains and lots of sailors
With lots of seaweed and slimy things on.
I saw something I had not yet seen; it had lots of legs and little eyes
I didn't think it wanted me there
So I swam as fast as I could,
I couldn't see it anymore.
I saw a string of pearls bubbling at my side,
Those pearls were my breath,
I could see the boat,
I thought it was time for me to go back.

Lucy Steel (10)
Orchard Close, Sibford School

An Encounter With An Octopus

I dived into the deep blue ocean,
It was a beautiful sight,
But over there in the corner,
Something caught my eye,
I crept down towards the thing,
The sand felt soft,
The thing was orange,
Could it be gold?
No,
It had eyes,
I know, it was the other diver,
I swam over to greet him,
He shot in front of me,
This was no man, it was an octopus!
It dived into my face,
It felt like a vacuum cleaner!
It was strong,
But I got away,
I swam for my life,
The octopus grabbed my wet leg,
Oh no!
This is it I was doomed,
Slowly I fell onto the sand,
There was no hope, I was
History!

Jacob Bearman (10)
Orchard Close, Sibford School

Me Diving

Plop! I go into dark blue sea.
Shiny cover on fishes
I'm following the fishes but creeping behind them
There's a blurry shadow.
Fish hiding behind scaly coral
I'm sneaking to the fizzy shadow.
Rotten food everywhere.
Vanish
The shadow has gone.
There it is again
Shark's teeth are like knives of steel.
I spring as fast as I can.
Fishes have popped out
Swirling around me like a tornado.
Crabs keep zooming in and out in the squashy sand.
All of a sudden.
Light
In the middle of the sea.
I swim
Dolphins spring up like pogo sticks.
I follow the dolphins.
Where am I?
I spring off a spiky rock and . . .
I'm showing myself on top of the ocean
Fresh air
Fizzing sand
Demanding people getting suntans
Now the cool summery ice cream.
Back to my comfortable home.

Kate Bowen (10)
Orchard Close, Sibford School

Dolphins

Dolphin jump
Dolphin swim
Oh you lively thing!

Dolphin jumping in the air,
Land on the sand bed all so fair.

  D ivine!
  O h so lively!
  L ively!
  P layful!
  H elen is their lover!
  I ntelligent!
  N ice!
  S o sweet!

Dolphin jumping in the air,
Land on the sand bed also fair.

Dolphin jump
Dolphin swim
Oh you lively thing!

Helen Bonham (8)
Orchard Close, Sibford School

Blenheim Palace

I had a thought
What would it be like to own
Blenheim Palace?
Gold plate and silver cups;
Paintings of queens,
Glistening chandeliers
Handsome gardens - a pony too.
I think about it . . .
How about you?

Katherine Bell (8)
Orchard Close, Sibford School

Searching Through The Desert

I am standing in the desert
with nowhere to go
miles and miles of nothing
but me in this lost world
the only thing to comfort me
is the sand below my warm feet.
I think I can see an oasis
or is it a dream in my head
I better go and see
yes! It is real
I will have a drink!
I will keep on looking
to discover what I desire!
I will keep on searching
until my life is over.

William Harrison (8)
Orchard Close, Sibford School

An Encounter With An Octopus

Down, down, down
A strange suction noise
I follow, follow, follow
A shipwreck
The noise is getting
Louder, louder, louder.
An octopus which is covering a body who's
Struggling, struggliing, struggling
Oh no it's coming to me
Agh!
Bubble, bubble, bubble
No more.

Henry Moore (10)
Orchard Close, Sibford School

Dogs And Kittens

D ogs are great
O vercome with love
G ood at running
S o sleepy and cuddly.

A nd we cannot leave out guinea pigs
N ow there are a lot of guinea pigs
D ig guinea pigs do!

K ittens are cute
I t's fun to have a kitten
T o have two kittens is more fun
T en kittens is hard work
E at a lot kittens do
N oisy, comfortable kittens
S o soft and warm to hold.

John Rafter-Tunnicliffe (9)
Orchard Close, Sibford School

Tigers! Tigers! Tigers!

Tigers are orange with black stripes.
Tigers sound like this, *(roar!)*
Tigers feel soft because of their fur.
Tigers taste like curry powder.
Tigers remind me of my second worst nightmare.
Tigers smell like cats.
Tigers are like large cats with stripes.
I've seen a real tiger.
I wanted a photo but I had no camera with me!

Jack Corrigan (8)
Radley CE Primary School

A Tiger

A tiger is as yellow as the sun,
A tiger feels like a teddy,
It smells like danger,
Its teeth are as sharp as needles.
A tiger's eyes are as round as a football,
A tiger's tail is as long as a snake,
A tiger is as scary as a spider.

Vicky Paige (7)
Radley CE Primary School

The Night Shadow

Creak, creak,
A shadow of black creeps through the moonlit house.
Creep, creep,
Creeping past our sleeping cat.
Scuffle, scuffle,
Scuffling across the squeaky floorboards.
It sounds like a terrible shuffling ghost,
Searching the house,
Seeking revenge.
The house goes silent and dark,
As a single mouse scuffles through our house.

Cara Doherty (9)
Radley CE Primary School

Have You Seen My Tiger?

It looks stripy like a zebra,
The colour is black and orange.
It smells like danger,
My tiger feels like fire,
It reminds me of a cat,
It sounds like a lion
And it tastes like tiger curry!

Chloe Busby (7)
Radley CE Primary School

Is It There?

It's in the air,
You can't see it
Just stop and stare,
It's as clear as water
It won't be there.

It sounds like the sea
Whooshing and waving,
Have you got the key
To the door of imagination?

It's wonderful,
It's sky-blue
But when you
Grow up . . .

It won't be there!

Bethan Rae Reeves Long (9)
Radley CE Primary School

Elephant

An elephant reminds me of an earthquake
When it stomps around.
It's got grey skin like a big stormcloud.
It roars like the siren of a boat
It tastes like rotten old meat.
Its skin is as rough as sand.
Elephants smell like stinky old garbage
And look like giant rocks with legs.

Thomas Harris (9)
Radley CE Primary School

My Best Mate Jake

My best mate Jake
Always likes to eat cake.
But he got fat
And sat on the cat.
The cat got flat
But Jake was still fat.
He weighed a tonne
Because he had too much fun.
He was bouncing around
Then he fell to the ground.
That was the last thing
He did to get thin.

Jonathan Charalambous (8)
Radley CE Primary School

Jamie Pies

Jamie Pies,
Often told lies,
But this was the worst of the lot,
Sadly this lie got him shot!
He lied about his military skills,
Face to face with Commander Hills.
He told so many of those lies,
But it took him by surprise,
That he got sent to war,
To help the Polish defend Warsaw.
And this is where our story ends,
I'm very sad to say my friends,
That poor old Jamie Pies got shot,
Gone but certainly not forgot!

Harvey Ball (9)
Radley CE Primary School

Mr Bear

Mr Bear ripped his hair
When putting on his underwear.
His head was so bald
He caught a cold.
He took to his bed
And then he was dead.

You readers take good care
When putting on your underwear!

Harry Sudworth (8)
Radley CE Primary School

A Python

It feels like a long soft pillow
It sounds like it's hissing a warning
It looks like it's going to attack its predator
The colour is black, grey and pink
It reminds me of an elastic band
It tastes like fear and a dry mouth
It smells like death to me.

Kyle Kerby (8)
Radley CE Primary School

A Tiger

Two adventurers went out one day
One jumped up and ran away
For he had spotted a black and orange creature.
Many birds were hiding in trees,
Many bees were leading their troops away
But the adventurer stood there thinking away
Of wonders in jungles when . . .
Roar!
The creature pounced
While the adventurer flounced . . .
For the creature was a tiger.

Conor Mosedale (7)
Radley CE Primary School

The Pebble's Journey

I am a pebble quickly bouncing on the river bed.
Crashing, tiny, pebble running down the mountain.
Squealing, moaning, jumping all the time.
Never looking back the deadly river killer.
I wonder why the river pushes and pulls all day long.
Never resting, never stopping.
Just to see the view.

Rory McLaughlin (10)
St Leonard's Primary School, Banbury

I Am The Pebble

I am the pebble
who saw the seas
I am the pebble
who travelled through trees.

I am the pebble
who jumped up and down
I am the pebble
who hit the ground.

I am the pebble
buried under the sand
who once saw the seas
splash on the land.

Anna Holmes & Elise Cole (9)
St Leonard's Primary School, Banbury

Pebble

I lived in the mountains,
Way up high
But one day I fell,
Down, down, down.
I landed with a splash,
I tumbled over rocks,
Crash!
And twirled down a waterfall.
At last calm, calm water,
Slowly I drifted down like a used sweet wrapper,
And there I stayed in peace.

Isabel Stafford (10)
St Leonard's Primary School, Banbury

Pebble

I go rushing down the river
crashing into rocks.
The water is pushing me to the edge.
I'm going very fast down the mountains.
I'm jumping underwater
flowing down to the bottom
swiftly, side to side.
I go rushing into mud
get horribly dirty.
I go so fast I cannot see
I go crashing into trees.
I've finally finished my journey.

Chantelle Merry-Taylor (10)
St Leonard's Primary School, Banbury

I Am A Pebble

I am a pebble
rushing down the mountains,
crashing into banks
and bumping into rocks.
Rumbling down waterfalls,
rolling fast through the forest
and bouncing on the sand river bed.
I twist round and round
through the water
then I come face to face
with the mouth.
Suddenly I'm separated
from my friend the river.

Emma Shaw (10)
St Leonard's Primary School, Banbury

Pebble's Journey

I like myself rolling down the stream on the mountain,
Meeting lots of my other friends.
Telling jokes, laughing and whispering secrets.
I like rolling down, down the waterfall,
Smashing boulders, swishing side to side,
Turning around into the meanders.
I like rolling, rolling down the river
Rushing, singing songs,
Getting away from my friends.
I like rolling down to the sea
Meeting strangers.

Hasib Iqbal (11)
St Leonard's Primary School, Banbury

My River

I am the pebble who lives who lives at the bottom of the sea
Who once lived in peace and harmony
I lived with the river, I lived with my friends
I thought that, that beautiful life would never end.
I miss the trees
I miss the cool summer breeze
I miss swinging up, I miss swinging down
Swinging and swinging all day long
I miss humans throwing sticks in the water
I miss racing them
So lonely, so cold
So sad, I have nobody
Oh how I wish that I was in the river swimming
Not sunk at the bottom of the seabed
I wish that I was in the river . . .
My river.

Sophie Louise McNally (9)
St Leonard's Primary School, Banbury

My Journey To The Sea

As I make my entrance
And come out from hiding
Out of the mountain from under the rocks
I start rushing down getting faster and faster
I am all alone
But then suddenly I am not on my own
I meet a friend and we rush down the mountain together
Now we are slowing down but we hit some rocks
Now we are falling
We are back on flat ground and getting faster
We are meandering, twisting and turning
But I am losing my friend, goodbye
Now I've come to my destination
I have finally reached the sea!

Bethany Packham (9)
St Leonard's Primary School, Banbury

The Pebble

I am the pebble
Who crashed its way
through the cracks and
down the mountain
and to the river
and down the waterfall
through the weeds.

I am the pebble
who glides across the sand
I see new creatures on my way.
I wish like the moon.

I am the pebble
who passed through the rubbish
I wish I could stay here
But the water tumbles me past
And I have to float.
On, on I go until I find the sea.

I am finally at the sea
And I am only half the size I used to be.

Harry O'Sullivan (9)
St Leonard's Primary School, Banbury

Rivers

I trickle down the rocks
And as I pick up speed,
I join other rivers,
Now I'm very big indeed.

As I splash and splash,
My depth begins to grow,
The sun shines on me,
My skin begins to glow.

As I pick up stones,
And run upon the land
Factories who empty toxic waste,
Try to make their grand.

As I become enraged,
I flood through towns and cities.
I upset a lot of people,
I think I drowned some kitties.

As I meander
I begin to calm.
I cut through the countryside,
I pass a large farm.

I am near my destiny,
I am heading south,
I think of my fate,
I have entered the mouth.

I am near the sea,
Reaching my end,
But not to worry,
Happiness is round the bend.

Adam Bushell (11)
St Leonard's Primary School, Banbury

Rivers

As I rush down the mountain,
And then feel all the rain.
I get quicker and quicker,
As I turn to a meander.

Now I'm down the mountain,
I'm like a giant fountain.
Then I'm rushing and gushing,
I'm going so fast I'm churning.

As more tributaries meet me,
A lot more swimmers in me.
Then I fall with the waterfall,
I sometimes wish it was a wall.

I am still hammering down,
I feel like I'm brown.
I'm plunging like a bomb,
I wonder where fish are from.

Now people are building factories,
Knock them down please.
They're clogging and choking me,
Abusing me is their destiny.

Now I'm at my destiny,
And that is the sea.

Matthew Hawtin (10)
St Leonard's Primary School, Banbury

Life As A Pebble Going To The Sea

I am a pebble in a river
I get smashed around
I get crashed and bashed as well
I split in half sometimes
I hate getting stuck
Because of the boulders.

People throw rubbish at me
The water is slow now
I still go but the boulders don't
Now I don't get stuck
Now I am at the sea.

Ashley Keyes (9)
St Leonard's Primary School, Banbury

What's The Point?

What's the point in the government, they just sit there
doing nothing all day, how can they change the world
when they're destroying it?

What's the point in poverty just share the money equally,
let's give more than boxes of toys for Christmas
let's give them a life and a home.

What's the point in racism, that's what causes war and fights,
it's not about black or white, you don't need to kill
because of their race or colour.

What's the point in child cruelty, it is the worst thing that can
happen to you; you can hear their voices shouting, 'Stop it!'
over and over but one day it will be too late to help.

What's the point?

Joshua Kerby (11)
St Leonard's Primary School, Banbury